D1099304

First I win a contest that
makes me a TV star.
Then I get to do some of
the most awesome extreme
sports in the world. And my
two best friends get
to come along for the ride.
How lucky am I?

550 493 959

First published in Great Britain in 2005 by
RISING STARS UK LTD.
76 Farnaby Road, Bromley, BR1 4BH

First published in Australia by Scholastic Australia in 2004.
Text copyright © Philip Kettle, 2004.

A Black Hills book, produced by black dog books

Designed by Blue Boat Design
Cover photo: Blue Boat Design

All rights reserved.

No part of this publication may be reproduced, stored in a retrieval
system, or transmitted, in any form by any means, electronic, mechanical,
photocopying, recording or otherwise, without the prior permission of the
copyright owner.

For more information visit our website at:
www.risingstars-uk.com

British Library Cataloguing in Publication Data

A CIP record for this book is available from the British Library

ISBN 1 905056 44 3

Printed by Bookmarque Ltd, Croydon, Surrey

KIRKLEES CULTURAL AND LEISURE SERVICES	
550 493 959	
Askews	17-Oct-2005
	£3.99
HF	CUL40379

THE XTREME WORLD OF BILLY KOOL

by Phil Kettle

book:05 skydiving

RISING STARS

CONTENTS

SKYDIVING EQUIPMENT

Altimeter
An altimeter measures altitude so you know when you should release your parachute.

Harness
A harness secures your main and reserve parachutes safely to your back.

Helmet
An aerodynamic helmet is worn for safety in case an accident occurs.

Jumpsuit
Skydiving jumpsuits are made with small wings to control the direction of your free fall.

Main Parachute

The main parachute is released to slow your fall and float you safely to the ground.

Reserve Parachute

If your main parachute fails, your reserve parachute is a backup.

Gloves

Gloves will be needed once your parachute is open so you can grip the steering cords.

Goggles

Goggles will reduce the pressure of cold wind in your eyes.

BASHER BROWN

I really like it when winter finishes.
There always seems to be more
time to do things in spring. The days
last longer.

Most afternoons, Sally, Nathan
and I end up at the park.

It isn't really a park. It is just an
odd-shaped block of land left over
after all the houses were built.

About three years ago the kids in
the neighbourhood made a cricket
pitch in the middle of the park.

Cricket made all the kids in the neighbourhood friends.

The best cricketer around is Basher Brown. Basher Brown's real name is John Brown. Sally called him 'Basher' after he hit the first ball he faced straight into the monster's backyard. John became Basher and I think after that we all forgot that he had any other name.

Basher isn't just good—he's great. He never tells us that he is better at cricket than we are. He doesn't have to—we all know he is. I would love to be as good at cricket as Basher, but I never will be. Basher is the best cricketer that I have ever seen.

He makes all the best teams and I have no doubt that one day he will play test cricket. Basher is a cricket fanatic. It's the only thing that he ever talks about.

Nathan reckoned that one day we would be able to talk about how we used to play cricket with Basher Brown.

I like doing extreme sports more than anything else. But if I wasn't hosting my TV show, *The Xtreme World of Billy Kool*, I would really like to be as good at cricket as Basher.

I'm not sure who first called the park Basher Park, but now that's the only name it is known by.

Basher Park is surrounded by the

back fences of houses. A really good hit straight down the pitch and over the bowler's head will land the ball in the monster's backyard.

The monster is the dog that lives behind the fence we pass every afternoon on the way home from school. Most games end with the ball going over the fence. Next day we all turn up again at the park and someone will have another ball.

None of us have ever seen the monster, other than his feet under the fence. But we have all heard his roar. That is scary enough. There is no doubt—the monster has to be the biggest dog in the world.

The big tree near the fence has

forty-three notches carved into it. Each notch represents a cricket ball that has been hit into the monster's backyard. Every notch belongs to Basher. Nobody else has managed to hit a ball far enough to clear the fence. Once, one of my balls hit the fence. That was the closest that I ever got to hitting the ball over the fence.

THE DARE

When I went to the park on Monday afternoon, Sally, Basher and Nathan were already there. Sally was telling Basher about the extreme sport that was coming up.

'We're going skydiving this weekend,' she said.

'You mean that you're going to jump out of a plane and try to beat it back to the ground,' Basher said as he twirled his cricket bat.

'Yeah, Basher, that's what we're

going to do,' said Nathan, who like me hadn't said much. There never was much time to say anything when Sally was trying to explain something!

'So you guys are going to jump out of a plane?' Basher asked as though he was having trouble taking it in.

'Yeah, that's right,' said Sally.

'Well, I reckon that would be pretty simple to do. I reckon that it would be scarier facing a really fast bowler,' Basher said. 'Yeah, I reckon that jumping out of a plane would be real easy.'

'I don't think it's going to be scary,' Sally said. 'But it's going to be the best adrenaline rush.'

I knew that I would rather jump from a plane than have to face a ball bowled by Basher. Not only was Basher the best batsman that I had ever seen, Basher was also a really fast bowler. Seeing a cricket ball leave Basher's hand, then turn into a blur as it travelled toward you … well, that was scary!

'Basher, I don't reckon you'd be game enough to do a parachute jump,' Nathan said to Basher.

Basher looked at Nathan. 'Well, I reckon that I'd have no trouble doing a parachute jump. It would be as easy as hitting a ball bowled by you over the fence.'

Sally and I didn't say anything.

We both knew that Basher could hit anything that we bowled to him straight over the fence. He had already done that to me lots of times.

Nathan sometimes spoke before he thought about what he was going to say. This was one of those times. He said, 'Basher, I'm going to ask the producer of our show if you can be a guest star on the next show.'

GOOD IDEA

The producer thought it was a great idea to ask one of our friends to come onto the show.

'It would show that other people are able to do extreme sports, not just you three,' he said. 'Bring him to the cast and crew meeting with you.'

The next afternoon we met at the park. Basher was already playing cricket with some of the other kids when we arrived.

'So, am I allowed to come?' asked

Basher as we walked to middle of the park.

'Yes,' said Nathan. 'You have to come to the cast and crew meeting with us on Friday.'

'That's cool.' Basher had a big smile on his face.

But then Nathan said something that I felt sure that he would regret. And that it was something that not only Nathan would regret, but Sally and me as well.

'Yeah, Basher, you're allowed to come, but you have to earn the privilege.'

Sally and I looked at each other. That was something that we hadn't discussed. Before we could say anything, Nathan spoke again.

'I'm going to bowl to you, and if you can hit one of the first three balls I bowl over the fence into the monster's backyard, you can come.'

'If I do that and I jump from the plane with you, then you should have to do something too,' said Basher.

'Like what?' said Nathan.

'Like going over the fence into the monster's backyard and getting all the cricket balls that have been hit there.'

'Wow, Nathan, you might just be about to do your last extreme sport.' Sally started to laugh.

'Nathan, I reckon you should

just tell Basher that he's allowed to come,' I said.

Nathan picked up the cricket ball from the ground and started to walk to the pitch. 'You've got a deal, Basher,' Nathan said.

Basher walked out to the pitch. Sally and I walked as close to the monster's fence as we were game to.

Nathan bowled the first ball. All the other kids started to cheer for Basher. Basher just played it straight back along the pitch to Nathan.

Nathan must have thought that he had a chance of stopping Basher from hitting the ball over the fence.

Nathan bowled again.

Basher stepped up to the pitch and

smashed the ball. The ball sailed straight over Nathan's head. Nathan shaded his eyes with his hand so he could see the ball. Sally, Nathan and I watched the ball as it sailed high over our heads, over the monster's fence. Thump. Not only did it go over the monster's fence, but it landed on the roof of the house, then rolled back into the yard. There was a roar from the monster, then silence. Maybe the monster was eating the cricket ball.

Nathan and Basher walked back to where we were standing.

'Well, that's me booked to go skydiving, and that's you over the fence to get all the cricket balls. I know that there are forty-four balls in there and you have to get the lot.'

'After you've done the skydive this weekend, we'll get them all,' Nathan said.

'What do you mean "we"?' I asked.

'We're a team aren't we?' Nathan said.

Getting those cricket balls was certainly going to be an extreme test of our courage.

CAST AND
CREW MEETING

On Friday afternoon the limo picked
us all up to go to the cast and crew
meeting. Basher was really excited.
He leaned back into his seat and
said, 'I could get used to this.'

'Don't forget, the deal was for one
show only,' Nathan said.

'Maybe they'll like me so much,
they'll invite me back,' Basher said.

'Don't count on it,' Nathan said.

When we got to the studio, we
went into the meeting room. The

director and the camera crew
were all huddled around the table
talking about something. They
were concentrating as hard as we
did when we faced up to Basher's
bowling.

'What's going on?' I asked.

The director said, 'We're trying to
figure out how we're going to shoot
the skydive. Two of the camera
crew are experienced skydivers
and they'll jump with you wearing
special helmets that have a camera
attached. We'll also have a camera
on the plane and one on the ground
to shoot footage of you landing.
You'll also be wired for sound. It's
just a bit tricky.'

The director pointed to a map on the wall. There was a drawing of a plane at the top of the piece of paper, then little stick figures joined to parachutes falling. Even on a sheet of paper, it looked like a long way down. I caught Basher looking at it. He'd turned kind of pale. Come to think of it, I think I had too.

'We'll pick you up at 9 o'clock,' the director said. 'It'll take an hour to get to the drop zone.'

Location Map

1. Plane reaches jumping altitude of 12 000 feet

2. Cameras are mounted on skydiver's helmets and wrists

3. Experienced skydivers shoot footage of the tandem jump

4. Sound and film crew operate from the ground at the drop zone

Our Equipment

Altimeter

Harness

Helmet

Jumpsuit

Main Parachute

Reserve Parachute

Gloves

Goggles

*BILLY, NATHAN, SALLY and
SHEY stand next to a small
plane at the drop zone.
BASHER BROWN is with them,
looking nervous.*

BILLY
Hi, welcome to another
show of *The Xtreme World
of Billy Kool*. I'm Billy
Kool and today my co-hosts
and I are at the drop
zone. Behind us is the
plane that we're going to
jump from. We are about
to go skydiving. Skydiving
is one of the most popular
extreme sports in the
world.

SALLY
Hi to all our viewers.
It's great to be here

today. Skydiving is going to be really cool.

NATHAN
You're right about skydiving being really cool, Sally. Especially when the plane gets up to 12 000 feet and the temperature outside is five degrees.

BILLY
Some days, the air temperature up there is so mild you can jump in shorts and a T-shirt. But not today. Our safety co-ordinator, Shey, is with us as usual. She's going to tell us everything we need to know about skydiving.

SHEY
Hi, everyone.

NATHAN
And as well as Shey, we
also have a special guest
who just happens to be our
friend, Basher Brown.

BASHER
Hi. Thanks for having me
on the show.

SALLY
Basher is a very good
cricketer. But today we
are going to find out how
he likes the adrenaline
rush of extreme sports.
Are you looking forward
to jumping out of a plane,
Basher?

BASHER
Right now I think I would rather be facing the fastest bowler in the world.

NATHAN
You don't have to do it if you don't think you can!

BASHER
There's no way I'm going to change my mind.

BILLY
The best thing about extreme sports is that anybody can do them.

SHEY
That's right, Billy. But you must have the right equipment and the right instructors. Safety is

very important. Extreme
sports can be very
dangerous.

NATHAN
Yeah, that's true. Did you
hear that, Basher?

BASHER
So is getting into a yard
with a really wild dog!

SALLY
That's right, Nathan.
Getting into a yard with
a wild dog would be the
most stupid thing that you
could do.

BILLY
In a few minutes we'll
board the plane. When the
plane gets to 12000 feet,
we'll be jumping.

NATHAN
Everything on the ground
will look like tiny toys
from that height.

SALLY
We'll be so high in the
air that we won't even
be able to see people on
the ground. But as we
come down, we'll have a
fantastic view of the sea.
We're very close to the
beach.

BILLY
Before we leave the ground
we have to put on the
right clothes and safety
gear.

SALLY
We're about to put on
jumpsuits, goggles,

gloves, and helmets, and then we have to be fitted with our harnesses.

BILLY
None of us is an experienced skydiver. So, we're going tandem. That means that we're going to be attached with a harness to experienced jumpers.

BASHER
I'm really pleased about that. I thought for a minute I might be jumping with Nathan.

SHEY
If you aren't an experienced skydiver, you should always jump with a very experienced skydiver.

BILLY
It's time for us to board the plane.

SALLY
Then comes the best part-the jump. Before we release the parachutes, we're going to free fall for forty seconds.

NATHAN
We'll get to feel what it's like to fly.

BASHER
Or what it's like to be a cricket ball about to hit the fence.

Billy, Sally, Nathan, Basher, and Shey board the plane. Most of the camera crew also board.

Some of them are wearing helmets with cameras attached so they can film the jump. They are called camera flyers. Finally, the skydiving instructors board. Billy and the others will be jumping in tandem with them. The plane takes off and begins climbing to 12000 feet.

BILLY
Here we are in the plane. We have all our gear on and in a few minutes we'll jump. I'm starting to feel a bit nervous!

SALLY
I'm not nervous. I'm really starting to feel the adrenaline flow. How

are you feeling, Basher?

BASHER
I'm not sure if it's
adrenaline flowing
around in my stomach,
but something is running
around there, that's for
sure.

NATHAN
You don't have to jump if
you don't want to.

BASHER
I'm jumping.

*The plane approaches the
right height. All the
harnesses and equipment
are checked again. Nathan,
Sally, Billy and Basher's
harnesses have been
attached to the harnesses*

worn by the skydiving instructors.

SHEY
We're ready to jump. How are you all feeling?

BILLY
When we look out the door of the plane, we can see a red circle on the ground—that's the drop zone, where we'll land.

NATHAN
It looks as small as a matchbox from up here.

The pilot turns around and yells out that the plane is in exactly the right position for the skydivers to jump.

SHEY
Are you ready to go?

BILLY
Sally said that she is going first.

SALLY
That's what you boys say every week. But I don't mind! See you on the ground.

The camera flyer exits the plane first and holds onto the outside of the aircraft. Without saying anything else, Sally and her partner jump straight out the door of the plane. The camera flyer lets go as they leave the plane. They jump together.

SALLY
Ahhhhhhhhhhhhhhh! I'm free
falling! This is amazing!

*Billy and his partner jump
next.*

BILLY
Ohhhhhhhhh...I think I left
my stomach in the plane!

*Nathan, Basher, Shey
and another camera flyer
follow Billy out of the
plane.*

BASHER
Ahhhhhhhhhhhhhhhhhhhhh!
This is great, but I think
I've left something in
the plane and it isn't my
stomach!

NATHAN
I'm a bird! I'm a bird!

SALLY
Yeah, a stone bird!

They free fall for forty seconds. Then the parachutes are released. After the opening shock—the jerk of the parachute opening—everyone starts floating towards the ground.

BILLY
We've just checked the altimeter. We're about 4500 feet in the air and floating toward the ground. This is awesome.

BASHER
I'm so pleased that I came. Anytime you want a guest on the show, let me know.

SALLY
I wonder whether Nathan
will have as much fun in
the monster's backyard.

NATHAN
I'm sure that we all will.

*Nathan does a fly-by. That
means that he 'flies' by
one of the camera flyers
who have been shooting the
jump.*

SHEY
That was the easy bit. Now
we've got to land. It's
good that the instructors
will be in control of the
landing, because it can be
difficult.

*They all land inside the
red circle. Billy, Basher*

*and Sally land perfectly.
Nathan and his jumping
partner turf-surf across
the ground and end up
out-landing. Shey falls to
the ground as though she's
jumped a hundred times
before.*

NATHAN
So that's what it's like
to be a bird. Can someone
help me out of this thing?
I'm all tangled.

SALLY
Can we go again?

SHEY
That was a great jump.
Time for the post-dive.
That's where we review the
jump and you all confess
how scared you were!

BILLY
That brings us to the
end of another fantastic
extreme sport. I've had
the best time. Until we
meet again at the site
of another extreme sport,
my name is Billy Kool and
you have been watching
*The Xtreme World of Billy
Kool.*

DIRECTOR
Cut! That's a wrap,
people. Well done.

BILLY
So who was scared?

NATHAN
I wasn't.

SALLY
Why do you never go first then?

BASHER
Yeah, Nathan. How come Sally has always got to go first?

NATHAN
I did go first at snowboarding. I try not to go first because it would be really sad if anything happened to me. So it's a lot better to try things on Sally first.

SALLY
You're my hero.

BILLY
Well, Nathan, we'll all
see how much of a hero you
are when you're getting
those cricket balls.

NATHAN
Whatever.

THE WRAP UP

It's been another unreal week. I wish I could have jumped by myself. Still, it was awesome even going tandem. Nathan is crazy for making that stupid bet. If Nathan thinks I'm going into the monster's backyard with him, then he's mistaken. I reckon I would be shaking so much I wouldn't even be able to get over the fence. Sally probably would, though. She's pretty brave.

Maybe we could throw lots of food in the backyard before Nathan gets over the fence. That might be the only way for him to survive.

Nathan's agreed to go into the monster's backyard before we go mountain biking in a couple of weeks. That's a long time to have a sick feeling in your stomach. If I was him, I wouldn't put it off. I'd go straight away. Maybe he's hoping that Basher will forget, but there's no way that will happen.

Dear Billy

My friend says that you use stunt doubles for your action shots. I don't think you do. Could you email me and tell me what really happens?

Thanks

Ryan, a fan

Extreme Information
History

People have always dreamed of being able to fly. The origins of the parachute have been traced back as far as the fifteenth century to Leonardo Da Vinci. Leonardo Da Vinci sketched a design of a parachute, but planes and hot-air balloons hadn't been invented then, so he had nowhere to test it.

In 1783, a Frenchman, Louis-Sebastien Lenormand, jumped from a tree in his quest to fly. To assist his flight he held two parasols—small umbrellas.

Another Frenchman, Jean Pierre Blanchard, designed and created the first silk parachute in 1785. The word 'parachute' means 'break fall'.

Andre-Jacques Garnerin was the first person to use a parachute regularly. He made the first exhibition jump from a hot-air balloon in Paris in 1797.

Parachuting from airplanes began in the later stages of World War I. It was used in World War II for combat and infiltrating agents into enemy territory.

The development of parachutes happened along three lines. First, to save the lives of pilots when they had to abandon their planes in the air. Second, to drop soldiers and equipment into battle zones. Third, as a sport or hobby.

Sport parachuting was established after World War II. In 1951, five countries competed in the first parachuting competition in Yugoslavia. Parachuting was recognised as a sport in 1954.

Since then, people have also been trying to fly, as well as to float safely to the ground with their parachutes.

'Bird' men and women have been trying to 'fly' during the period of free fall before they release their parachutes.

In the beginning, they made 'wingsuits' out of canvas, wood and metal. Wingsuits are now made out of highly advanced materials, yet the sport is still very dangerous. Many bird men and women have died.

Tandem jumping became popular in the 1980s and opened up skydiving to a lot of people. It is a very popular extreme sport.

Glossary

Base jump

A jump made from a fixed object rather than an aircraft. BASE stands for Building, Antennae, Spans (bridges) and Earth (cliff).

Camera flyer

A free fall photographer equipped with a camera fastened to their helmet.

Canopy

Another word for a parachute.

Cut away

If the main parachute fails, it needs to be 'cut away' before the reserve parachute is released. This stops the two parachutes getting tangled. It is 'cut away' by releasing a lever on the jumper's harness.

Dirt dive

Practising manoeuvres on the ground before the jump takes place.

Drag

Being pulled by the parachute while on the ground.

Drop zone

A skydiving centre or the area where skydivers land.

Feet

A unit of length used in skydiving to describe the height of the jump.

Fly-by

Flying by a camera, either in free fall or under the parachute.

Free fall

The period after you jump from the plane before deploying the parachute. The fall speed builds up an air cushion on which the skydiver soars. Some skydivers say that free fall is the best part of skydiving because it doesn't feel like falling—it's more like flying.

Opening shock

The jerk skydivers feel when their parachute opens.

Out-landing

Landing off target.

Post dive

A review of a skydive after everyone has landed.

Skysurfing

Skydiving with a skyboard attached to the skydiver's feet (similar to a snowboard).

Turf-surf

Skimming centimetres above the ground for the last twenty to thirty metres under the parachute.

Equipment

Parachutes

Skydivers carry a main parachute and a reserve parachute when they jump. The parachutes are housed in a container that is worn like a backpack and harnessed to the body. The reserve parachute is used in an emergency where the main parachute fails to open. Because of this, reserve parachutes are packed under extremely strict regulations.

Parachute canopies are usually made of zero-porosity nylon fabric that lasts for a long time.

No parachute is 100% reliable. Poor packing and pre-jump inspection are usually the causes of parachute malfunctions.

Jumpsuits

Jumpsuits are not essential, but different fabrics, designs and sizes help skydivers control descent speeds and their free fall. Tight, slippery materials make for a faster fall rate. Larger jumpsuits made of non-slippery materials give a slower fall rate.

Altimeters

Visual altimeters show the skydiver what altitude they are at. They are worn on the wrist or chest. Audible altimeters with pre-set alarms are worn near the ears to aid in altitude awareness. They beep at a pre-set altitude to tell the skydiver how high they are.

Helmets

Student jumpers and most experienced jumpers wear helmets. For experienced jumpers, helmets range from leather aviator-style hats to full-coverage hard helmets, made especially for skydiving.

Goggles

Jumpers wear goggles or sunglasses to protect their eyes from freefall speeds of more than 190 kilometres per hour. They keep wind and grit out of the eyes.

PHIL KETTLE

Phil Kettle lives in inner-city Melbourne, Australia. He has three children, Joel, Ryan and Shey. Originally from northern Victoria, Phil grew up on a vineyard. He played football and cricket and loved any sport where he could kick, hit or throw something.

These days, Phil likes to go to the Melbourne Cricket Ground on a winter afternoon and cheer on his favourite Australian Rules team, the Richmond Tigers. Phil hopes that one day he will be able to watch the Tigers win a grand final—'Even if that means I have to live till I'm 100.'

THE XTREME WORLD OF BILLY KOOL

by Phil Kettle

Billy Kool books are available from most booksellers.
For mail order information please call Rising Stars on 01933 443862 or visit www.risingstars-uk.com